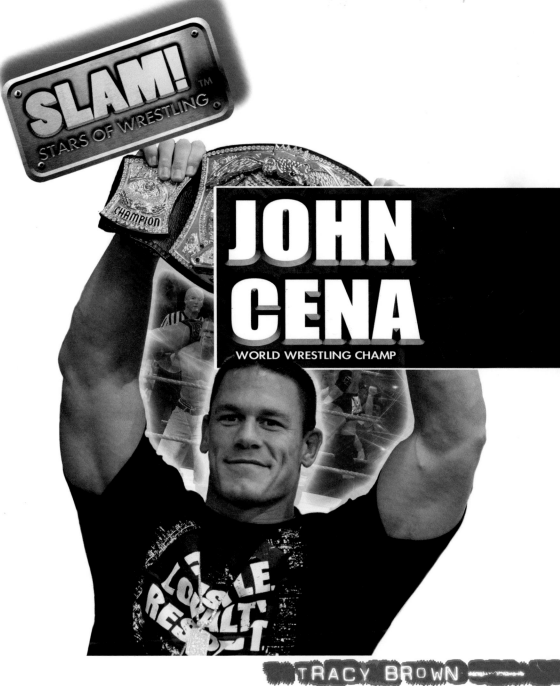

SLAM!™
STARS OF WRESTLING

CHAMPION

JOHN CENA

WORLD WRESTLING CHAMP

TRACY BROWN

rosen publishing's
rosen
central®

New York

For Eamonn

Published in 2012 by The Rosen Publishing Group, Inc.
29 East 21st Street, New York, NY 10010

First Edition

Library of Congress Cataloging-in-Publication Data

Brown, Tracy.
John Cena: world wrestling champ/Tracy Brown.
    p. cm.—(Slam! stars of wrestling)
Includes bibliographical references and index.
ISBN 978-1-4488-5534-6 (library binding : alk. paper)—
ISBN 978-1-4488-5593-3 (pbk. : alk. paper)—
ISBN 978-1-4488-5594-0 (6-pack : alk. paper)
1. Cena, John—Juvenile literature. 2. Wrestlers—United States—Biography—Juvenile literature. I. Title.
GV1196.C46B76 2012
796.812092—dc23
[B]
                                                                            2011022614

Manufactured in the United States of America

CPSIA Compliance Information: Batch #W12YA: For further information, contact Rosen Publishing, New York, New York, at 1-800-237-9932.

On the cover: A proud John Cena holds up a championship belt following a press conference that was held in the Ariston Theatre, San Remo, Italy, March 2006.

CONTENTS

INTRODUCTION

Nobody could have guessed that John Cena, as a scrawny twelve-year-old growing up in West Newbury, Massachusetts, would become one of the best-known and best-loved wrestlers in World Wrestling Entertainment, Inc. (WWE). This success did not come easily. Cena was not born with physical strength or inherent popularity. In fact, he was an outcast whose love for hip-hop culture made him the brunt of teasing when he was a young boy. His thin frame made him an easy target for bullies. To protect himself, he worked hard to build his body, which led to a lifelong love of athleticism and fitness.

Cena did not fit in well with the other kids in his small town. Instead of conforming, he recognized at an early age that staying true to yourself is key to achieving your goals. Even in the ring today, John Cena is John Cena. He does not play outrageous characters that are wildly different from himself. His greatest gift has been this sense of confidence. Even as a kid, and in spite of the teasing, he always wore what he liked, listened to what he liked, and did what he liked.

He has truly lived by his well-known motto since day one: hustle, loyalty, and respect. Throughout his life, Cena has worked really hard to succeed at his goals, which have ranged from academic to athletic, musical to dramatic.

Cena is a film star, rap artist, world-famous athlete, college graduate, and happily married man (to his high school sweetheart). To date, he has won sixteen titles, including the WWE Championship seven times and the World Heavyweight Championship twice. He is a true champion, any way you slice it.

The Miz and John Cena battle it out during their WWE Championship match, WrestleMania XXVII, April 3, 2011, at the Georgia World Congress Center, Atlanta, Georgia.

1 EARLY LIFE

John Felix Anthony Cena was born on April 23, 1977, in West Newbury, Massachusetts. He was the second of five boys born to his parents, John and Carol Cena. His brothers are Dan, Matt, Sean, and Steve.

When John was a kid, he had a passion for hip-hop culture. He made up his own rhymes, dressed in hip-hop style, and loved rap music. He grew up in a small town where the rest of the kids were more into heavy metal. He was often teased because of his individual style and taste, but John always stayed true to himself.

Pumping Iron

Cena credits the teasing he suffered as a kid with his interest in weight lifting. He recalls being a unique kid, one who dressed a certain way and acted a certain way and didn't quite fit in with everybody around him. He was picked on a lot, especially around the ages of twelve and thirteen, when he started going to junior high school and mixed more with the older kids.

It's hard to believe, but Cena was a relatively small kid. He weighed only 125 pounds (57 kilograms) when he was in the seventh grade. When he was in junior high, he'd have to walk through the adjoined high school to get his bus at the end of the day. When he did, the older kids would beat him up. To protect himself from bullies, he decided to get bigger. When he was twelve, his father bought him a weight set.

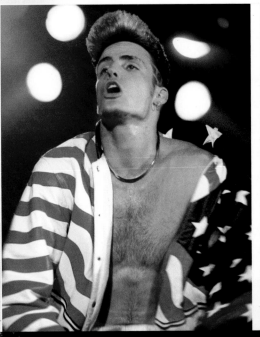

John Cena was a big fan of hip-hop culture, and it influenced his musical and fashion sense as a child and into adulthood. *(left,* Vanilla Ice; *right,* Will Smith*)*

He was passionate about lifting from the start. He had his first workout at twelve, and he hasn't missed one since. His hard work and commitment paid off. He went from 155 pounds (70 kg) to 215 (98 kg). When he graduated from high school, Cena weighed between 235 pounds (107 kg) and 250 pounds (113 kg). By then, the teasing had long stopped!

Wrestling Fanatic

Cena was interested in sports and fitness for reasons other than self-defense. His father was a huge wrestling fan and worked as an announcer for Chaotic

Wrestling, under the name John Fabulous. John's dad introduced his sons to the sport. It was one way that Cena bonded with his father and brothers.

While other boys played catch or tossed a football around with their dads, Cena and his brothers watched wrestling. His dad would go to events like his sons' Little League games, but he wasn't into baseball and had no idea what was going on. He didn't know any sports but wrestling.

They had cable television before anyone else in the neighborhood, so they could watch matches. He became a big fan of superstar wrestler Hulk Hogan.

But Cena didn't really participate other than as a fan and a spectator. In high school, he excelled at football, and later he was Division III All-American center in college football.

True to His Roots

Hulk Hogan is one of the best-known and best-loved stars of the WWE and later starred in the successful reality series *Hogan Knows Best.* He is one of John Cena's heroes.

Cena's father was a real hero to him. He learned from his dad's example how important it is to work hard for what you

OUTSIDE THE RING

Cena has interests outside of wrestling, too. Some of them may not be surprising: he collects sports jerseys and muscle cars, and likes to play video games. But he is also a fan of Japanese animation and has said that his favorite film in the genre is *Fist of the North Star*. His favorite sports teams are the Boston Red Sox and the New England Patriots.

want. According to About.com, "He was self-employed, self-made, and raised five sons," he recalls. "At a young age, and without sitting us down and browbeating us, he showed us that there is no substitute for hard work to succeed and get the things you want in life."

Even today, Cena remains down to earth. He drives a Hyundai, and he married his high school sweetheart in 2009. He has never forgotten the importance of family. He has used his fame to support his family in many ways.

In 2007, Cena and his four brothers attended Chaotic Wrestling's independent wrestling show. It was held in a small gym in Byfield, Massachusetts. John was there to help draw a crowd to raise awareness for an organization called MADD (Mothers Against Drunk Driving). This was an important event for the Cena family because John's brother Dan, who is a police officer, was once in a car accident caused by a drunk driver. John was able to use his celebrity to draw a crowd and help support a great cause.

John Cena, rapper and producer Freddie Foxx, and Cena's cousin, hip-hop artist and poet Tha Trademarc. Together they recorded John's rap album, called *You Can't See Me*, in 2005.

Cena has a close relationship with a distant cousin, rap artist Marc Predka, who is better known as Tha Trademarc. Not only have he and his cousin collaborated musically, but when Predka published a book of poetry in 2010, Cena went on Twitter to tell all his followers that the book was published and to celebrate his cousin's gift. "Marc, I am so proud of you," one tweet said. "It's brilliant."

No Pain, No Gain

Cena applied the commitment and work ethic that he learned from his dad to academics. He applied to sixty colleges and was accepted to fifty-eight. He chose to attend Springfield College in Springfield, Massachusetts.

In college, he was a star football player, but he did dabble in wrestling, taking it as an elective class. He was a physical education major, and as part of his coursework, he had to take a lot of electives in order to prepare him for a career teaching phys ed or coaching. He had to be a well-rounded athlete. He was a football player by trade. He also did a little bit of track in high school. Then for .5 credits, he learned the basics of amateur wrestling.

After studying hard and earning his degree in 1998, Cena still didn't know exactly what he wanted to do with his life. He was still passionate about physical fitness and weight lifting in particular. He was also determined to leave the town where he'd grown up. He has never been afraid of trying new things. He decided to move far from Massachusetts and pursue a career in bodybuilding. In 1999, he packed up and moved to California, eager to start a new adventure and face new challenges.

2 CALIFORNIA DREAMING

After graduating from college on the East Coast, John Cena decided to head west to California. He wasn't exactly sure what he wanted to do, but having just graduated with a degree in exercise physiology, it made sense that he would focus on applying his knowledge of the body and health to a career in athletics.

In particular, Cena was a savvy bodybuilder. He'd already had some amateur success, winning the teen division at a bodybuilding event in Newburyport, Massachusetts, just before heading to college. Two years later, he returned to the same event and won the men's tall class and overall titles.

His commitment to bodybuilding grew throughout his college years. While friends of his were off vacationing in Cancun, Mexico, during spring break, Cena found himself spending a week at a Gold's Gym in Venice, California. And that's exactly where he decided to return after graduation. He says the place just won him over. He moved to Venice, California, not to be a bodybuilder, per se, but just to be near Gold's Gym.

His dad, however, was not so pleased—or optimistic. As Cena recalled in *Men's Health* magazine in 2009, "My dad, who's a typical small-town guy, said I'd be back in two weeks. And that was enough for me." Cena truly blazed his own trail, heading west without a safety net or much of a plan. "I had two military duffle bags and $500," he told *Men's Health*. "No hook-ups, no place to stay, nothing. Just did what I had to do to get by."

Going for Gold

He was not exactly an overnight success. He took various jobs in California, including that of a limousine chauffeur. Most of his time, however, was spent at his beloved Gold's Gym. According to the *Men's Health* interview, it was worth all the hard knocks, and there were many. Cena lived in a garage at one point, and at another he lived in his car. But at the age of twenty-one, and with a passion for bodybuilding, he was exactly where he wanted to be.

Cena not only spent time working out at Gold's he also worked behind the counter. It was this job that introduced him to hopeful wrestlers who came in to train. A chance discussion with one gym regular encouraged Cena to give wrestling a shot. There's no doubt that Gold's Gym played a major role in Cena discovering himself as a wrestler. He later did a television advertisement for the gym that helped jump-start his career.

John Cena celebrates after winning the championship title at WrestleMania XXVI, March 28, 2010, which was held at the University of Phoenix Stadium in Glendale, Arizona.

John Cena strikes at his opponent, Batista, during a WWE Raw wrestling match, May 5, 2010, in Monterrey, Mexico. Batista is the longest-reigning World Heavyweight Champion in WWE history.

Training Camp

In 2000, Cena began training at Irvine, California-based Ultimate University, which was run by Ultimate Pro Wrestling (UPW). It was there that he learned to change his workout from that of a bodybuilder to that of a wrestler.

Ultimate University was a "feeder" school that trained wrestlers for careers in the WWE, as well as other wrestling federations. It has since disbanded, but within three years of its inception in 1998, thirteen of its wrestlers had made it to the WWE. Rick Bassman, who ran UPW, told *Wrestling Digest* in 2001 what it takes to be a WWE star. "If you're born into it, you have a leg up," he said. "But whether someone comes in with 'it' or not, they have to have the right attitude, know it's hard to make it, and be supportive of people."

Cena definitely had what it took. At UPW, he introduced his robotic character, the Prototype. He held the heavyweight championship for just under a month in April 2000, and the next year signed a contract with the World Wrestling Federation (WWF). He was sent to train at Ohio Valley Wrestling in Louisville, Kentucky, where he joined several other wrestlers in preparing for careers in the WWF. He trained really hard for a year, learning his stuff and impressing his coaches. In 2002, he was ready for his WWF debut.

Athletics Before Entertainment

Although WWE wrestling requires athletic skill, there is a large component of it that is intended to be entertaining. Many of the stunts are just that, choreographed and planned, as they would be in an action film. But Cena has stayed true to his roots, thinking of himself first and foremost as an athlete.

DRUG USE—NOT A GIVEN IN WRESTLING

The WWE and other wrestling associations have come under fire for encouraging the use of steroids, dangerous drugs that can temporarily enhance an athlete's performance and promote muscle growth. The pressure for wrestlers to perform while keeping up with strenuous schedules can also lead to the abuse of painkillers. But does being in the WWE and abusing medications go hand in hand? In a *USA Today* interview in 2004, Cena rejected the idea, saying, "Steroids and painkillers (aren't) a professional choice but a lifestyle. I've learned to play in pain. If it's a serious enough injury, I take time off." As for himself, Cena denied ever using a performance-enhancing drug, and that his build is the result of pure hard work. In 2009, he told *Men's Fitness*, "Train with me for just a week, and you'll see I'm the guy who drives 250 miles between shows, but will be at the gym tomorrow at 10 AM, when most people are sleeping in. I'm the guy who'll fly to Australia, find a gym, fly back, and the first thing I do off the plane is work out, before I even shower or eat. I've made a living out of working hard."

Indeed, WWE wrestlers need to be in good shape in order to keep up with their schedules and keep their bodies healthy as they endure sometimes-brutal matches. Professional wrestlers compete all the time. Unlike other athletes, they don't have sixteen games a year, or even eighty-one games a year. They do three hundred shows a year, so it's game day every day of the week.

Cena keeps himself in top shape. While there is no signature "John Cena workout," he likes to do a variety of workouts to work different parts of his body. He does a particular type of weightlifting with what are known as Olympic plates. Rather than using modern machines that you might see at your local gym, chains and boxes are used, for example. It takes a lot of skill to perform this kind of workout without injuring yourself.

In a FOX interview, Bum Jin Lee, a strength and conditioning specialist, talked about the importance of athletes training as hard as they perform. In wrestling, you have 250-pound (113 kg) guys making contact with each other. In order for them to bounce back up and go again, they have to train hard.

John Cena in the 2009 action film *12 Rounds*, in which he plays Danny Fisher, a New Orleans detective. Cena takes his acting very seriously, but he is first and foremost a wrestler.

Lee owns the gym where Cena worked out while making his 2009 movie, *12 Rounds*. Cena's choice of workout isn't available in many other gyms because it's simply too high risk. Lee describes the workout as hard work, but necessary.

Education First

Cena acknowledges a fair bit of luck that was involved in his becoming a WWE star. There is no guaranteed path that will lead to a career with the WWE. It's very much like acting or playing sports. Only 1 percent of the people who actually try out for it can say they make a living doing it. Cena advises young people to work hard in other areas of their life, which can only improve their success in whatever they try. He stresses to high school students that education must come first. Being a college graduate and having had a very prolific football career, sports entertainment wasn't really his first choice. He actually wanted to play football, but with his size and playing ability, he felt that college football was as far as he could go with it. It wasn't until after he finished his education that he seriously looked at sports entertainment as a way to make a career for himself.

3 RUTHLESS AGGRESSION

On June 27, 2002, the same year the WWF changed its name to World Wrestling Entertainment (WWE), John Cena made his SmackDown debut by accepting an open challenge from Kurt Angle.

According to youtube.com, from the ring, Angle called on any wrestler whom he'd never wrestled before to come out of the locker room and face him. "Come on guys, there's got to be someone back there who wants to seize the moment," he taunted, the crowd roaring and cheering. Nobody appeared ready to face him.

"There are a lot of guys back there," Angle continued, "future superstars, who are looking to climb the ladder to success. Well now's your chance to become a sensation, just like me." Again, nobody entered the ring. "Listen," he appealed, "don't be scared. I will take it easy on you." With that, the music began to blare and the lights flashed as Cena appeared in the stadium, ready to accept the challenge.

The announcer recognized Cena. He described him as a young talent who was looking to knock on the door of opportunity.

Angle was not impressed. The two men stared each other down in the center of the ring as Angle asked whom in the heck Cena thought he was. "I'm John Cena," Cena said, not batting an eye. Angle asked him to name the one quality he possessed that made him think he could come out into the ring and face the very best in the business. "Ruthless aggression," was Cena's answer, and he gave Angle a surprise smack.

John Cena's SmackDown debut was made when he was challenged by Kurt Angle *(top)*, shown here wrestling Eddie Guerrero in 2004. Cena lost the match but gained a lot of fan support.

Although Cena lost, he fought hard and it was a very close match. The crowd was impressed by his performance and his manner. When it was over, Angle refused to shake Cena's hand. The announcer commented that wrestling is all about class and sportsmanship, and he criticized Angle for his lack of both qualities. It was Cena's WWE debut, and he gained fan support almost immediately.

Early Feuds and Titles Won and Lost

Cena's career took off like a firecracker after his debut match against Kurt Angle. In particular, he had earned the respect of the Undertaker, a wrestler whose real name is Mark William Calaway. The Undertaker and Cena teamed up against Angle and Chris Jericho.

The Taker and Cena teamed up on July 11, 2002, at an event in Atlantic City, New Jersey. The Taker had gotten into a skirmish with Angle and Jericho, and he believed that Cena had bailed on him, leaving him to fight the two wrestlers himself. An angry Taker marched into the locker room and reminded Cena that he'd been around for only two weeks, whereas the Undertaker had been wrestling for twelve years. He demanded that Cena "have his back" in the ring at that night's event, and Cena agreed he would.

The four wrestlers fought what was the main event of the evening. During the match, Cena got Jericho in a surprise pin, holding his shoulders down on the mat. Jericho was so offended at being pinned by a rookie that he struck back hard. The two wrestlers battled over the next few months.

In 2004, Cena defeated the Big Show and won the U.S. Championship. He lost the title just four months later to Angle. However, he won it back again after a best-of-five match with Booker T. But this time, his reign

"KAYFABE" STABBED

While enjoying himself at a nightclub in Boston in 2004, John Cena was "kayfabe" stabbed in the kidney. "Kayfabe" is a term for the "secret" behind wrestling. Storylines and matches are presented as real but in fact are often scripted for entertainment value. In the "stabbing" incident, the culprit turned out to be the bodyguard of fellow wrestler Carlito Caribbean Cool. Cool was new on the WWE scene. He had made his debut not long before the stabbing. He and Cena were engaged in a feud, and the kayfabe stabbing was a way to keep the story alive outside of the ring. The "stabbing" meant that Cena had to take off a month to "heal," and during this time he shot his first movie, *The Marine*.

only lasted a week, and he surrendered the title to Carlito Caribbean Cool, prompting another feud.

True to His Character

Cena briefly played a character, the Prototype. He has also adopted the nickname "the Doctor of Thuganomics." For most of his career, however, he has been himself in the ring, rather than adopting personas that are wildly different from his own, as so many wrestlers do. Cena says that he is one of the lucky ones because his character in wrestling is basically just himself. He turns up the volume in front of twenty thousand people, but he is still basically his everyday self.

He credits staying true to his own character as one of the reasons for his popularity. He describes himself as a rebel, a regular dude with real attitude, and he thinks his fans can relate to that.

One of the aspects of himself that Cena was able to bring to the ring was his love of hip-hop music and fashion. For Halloween in 2002, he decided to dress up like rapper Vanilla Ice. He kept it up long after Halloween was over, and his gimmick was born: building an audience through rapping. He credits his rapping with his not being cut from the WWE in the early days. At the time, he was stronger at rapping than he was at wrestling, so he viewed it as a vehicle to help him make an

A victorious and pumped-up John Cena holds up his belt at WrestleMania XX, March 14, 2004, Madison Square Garden, New York City.

FACE VS. HEEL

In most wrestling storylines, a "face" is pitted against a "heel." The heel is the villain—the character the crowd is against, or the wrestler whose character is least likable. The face is the good guy—or at least a better guy than the heel. John Cena was a face throughout the early days of his career, starting with his offering his hand in respect to Kurt Angle after Cena's premiere match, which he lost. Angle refused to shake his hand, making Cena the more likable of the two.

In October 2002, Cena's image began to change, and he went from being a face to being a heel. He had been paired with Billy Kidman in a Tag Team Championship, and they lost. Cena began feuding with Kidman, blaming him for the loss, and his image changed to that of a bad guy. He also had feuds with Triple H and Rob Van Dam. But Cena has been a face for most of his career, with the occasional heel storyline.

impact. He saw it as his best tool for entertaining the public and putting him on the map. He tried to make sure that everything he said was the funniest and the most edgy stuff he could possibly say.

Cena went on to recall how his rapping helped him be an entertainer and gain a following, allowing him to develop his wrestling skills more fully. He felt it was a case of sink-or-swim for him at the start of his wrestling career, and he really wanted to succeed. He started to incorporate hip-hop into his act, and that at least showed everyone that he had something to say. From then on, match after match, he progressively worked on his craft and then hit a point in his career where he actually wanted to stop speaking and start wrestling. And that's exactly what he did.

4 WWE: 2005-2011

After John Cena recovered from his nightclub "stabbing," which was a storyline that allowed him to take time off to film his first movie, he was back in the ring. Among his first actions were to win back the U.S. Championship title and premiere the new "spinner" U.S. Championship belt. The belt had been altered to have a turntable in the front.

On January 30, 2005, he participated in the eighteenth Royal Rumble, a pay-per-view WWE event that took place in Fresno, California. In this match, Cena made it through to the final two, which pitched him against Batista. The winner would earn a place at WrestleMania XXI and a chance at either the WWE Championship or the World Heavyweight Championship. Batista won the match, but Cena got a second chance to make it to WrestleMania XXI a month later. This time, he defeated Kurt Angle to win his spot.

Chain Gang Soldiers

Cena won a place in the spotlight SmackDown event at WrestleMania XXI. He would go up against John "Bradshaw" Layfield (JBL). As soon as this was made public, the two wrestlers began a much-publicized feud. The feud cost Cena the U.S. Championship, which he lost to JBL's chief of staff, Orlando Jordan. After winning the title, Jordan and JBL "destroyed" the turntable belt that Cena had worn while champion, which made the feud even more heated.

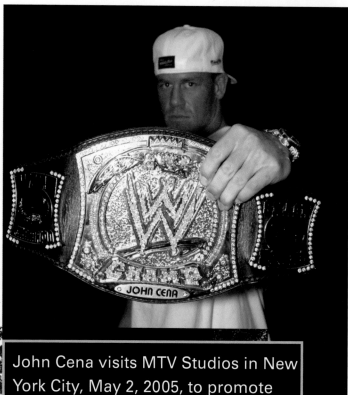

John Cena visits MTV Studios in New York City, May 2, 2005, to promote his rap album *You Can't See Me.* The album was well received.

Cena swore revenge, but was warned by Smack-Down general manager Teddy Long that he should not retaliate until the WrestleMania event. If Cena touched JBL before the event, he would lose his place. What followed was a series of attacks on JBL's property, including the tires of his limousine being slashed and his ten-gallon hat being destroyed.

During a match between JBL and another wrestler, Cena interfered and threatened JBL with a chair. Instead of smashing JBL and losing his WrestleMania shot, he sat on the chair, looked down at JBL, and made his "You can't see me" gesture. During this feud with JBL, Cena established a name for his core of fans, the Chain Gang Soldiers, and he himself began to be called the Chain Gang Soldier.

The Top of the WWE World

At last on April 3, 2005, at the Staples Center in Los Angeles, California, it was time for Cena to face JBL in the ring at WrestleMania XXI. He defeated

John Cena is surrounded by adoring fans and eager photographers at WrestleMania XXI, Staples Center, Los Angeles, California, April 3, 2005. Cena is appreciative of his fans and doesn't like to let them down.

JBL and became the WWE Champion, but the feud didn't end there. Cena once again altered the championship belt into a turntable design, and JBL continued to wear his title belt, still proclaiming to be the champion. But Cena had arrived at the top of the WWE world!

He would confirm his dominance over JBL at the next SmackDown event, "Judgment Day," which took place on May 22, 2005, at the Target Center in Minneapolis, Minnesota. This match would be what is called an "I quit" match, which is one in which the only way to win is to get your opponent to say the words "I quit" into the microphone. This kind of match is typically organized to end a long feud or rivalry, the idea being that having to verbally admit defeat clearly establishes one wrestler as stronger than the other, and the feud ends.

Cena lost the WWE Championship in January 2006, but quickly won it back within the same month. He lost it again in June, but he regained it and entered 2007 as the champion.

Injured and Ringside

On October 2, 2007, Cena had an unscripted, legitimate injury. During a match with Mr. Kennedy, he completely tore his pectoral muscle, a fan-shaped muscle in the chest area. He told the *Sun* how it happened in a 2008 interview, recalling that it happened with a hip-toss maneuver, which is like a Judo-based hip throw.

After the injury, he stayed in the ring for a scripted fifteen-minute attack from Randy Orton. "I don't think it helped matters that I stayed in the ring for another fifteen minutes and got whipped by Randy Orton afterwards," Cena told the *Sun*, "but I think, all things considered, it tore clean off—I couldn't have done any more damage to it. Sometimes I'm blind with pride and I take my profession very seriously, and I know people paid good money to see me perform that night, and as long as I didn't move my right arm, I was capable of performing. So that's what I did."

His injury took seven months to heal, during which time he had to surrender his championship and observe ringside. Being out of the game when he was at the top was difficult for Cena, a dedicated performer and competitive athlete, but he wasn't resentful or bitter. "I actually watched the footage

K-Fed

One of the most bizarre feuds that Cena had was with Kevin Federline. Federline is a rapper known as K-Fed, but he is most famous for being the ex-husband of pop singer Britney Spears. In 2006, Federline was promoting his album, *Playing with Fire*. To give him exposure, the WWE involved him in a few fictional storylines, called angles. On October 16, 2006, he bumped up against Cena, having minor physical altercations but no official match. But a week later, on October 26, Federline slapped Cena very hard in the face, prompting a feud. On November 6, Federline challenged Cena to an official match at the New Year's Day Raw event. Cena accepted, and to the surprise of many, lost the match to Federline.

for the first time yesterday. They had it on an Italian program," he went on to say in the same interview. "And when the whole thing was over, I was just more upset with myself because it was right before a Last Man Standing match with me and Randy. He's one heck of a competitor; we really have some great matches in the ring. It's something that I wanted to do, and it just didn't work out that way. I was definitely more upset with myself than anybody else."

On January 27, 2008, Cena made a surprise return to the ring. At the Royal Rumble, which took place in Madison Square Garden in New York City, he won the WrestleMania title shot. It was a triumphant return to the ring after sitting out so many months while his pectoral muscle healed. Unfortunately, he did not remain injury-free for long. In August 2008, he suffered a herniated disk in his neck, which requires surgery to heal. He again left until

Aspiring rapper and Britney Spears's ex-husband Kevin Federline wrestles John Cena, January 1, 2007. Federline was promoting his first album, *Playing with Fire*.

November. His return was characteristically strong: he defeated Chris Jericho for his first-ever World Heavyweight Championship.

Fired/Rehired

In November 2010, Cena was the guest referee at a match that would, according to the storyline, decide his own fate as a professional wrestler. In the main event of the Survivor Series, Orton was pitted against Wade Barrett. If Orton won, according to the storyline, Cena would be fired from the WWE. Orton lost that match, and Cena's firing was announced. It was unclear of course whether this firing was real or whether it was just a cover story to free Cena up to film his next motion picture.

Cena was back in the ring a month later and was "rehired." He went on to win the WWE Championship match at WrestleMania XXVII.

5 LIFE OUTSIDE THE RING

John Cena has applied his motto of "Hustle, loyalty, and respect" to everything he's ever done. Hard work, dedication, and unwavering drive have ensured his success in the wrestling ring, but he has achieved a lot in other areas as well. He has also made a name for himself as an actor and rap artist.

You Can't See Me

Music has always been a big part of Cena's identity. Since childhood, he has been drawn to hip-hop culture. He has been listening to rap music and writing his own rhymes since he was just a kid. His admiration for rap artist Vanilla Ice inspired his rapper personality in the WWE. But while Cena has incorporated his rap skills into wrestling, he left wrestling out of his music when he recorded his first album.

The album, which was released in May 2005, is called *You Can't See Me*, a reference to his famous hand-swiping gesture that he uses to intimidate opponents. But other than the name of the album, Cena did not incorporate his wrestling personae into his lyrics. Other rappers have made that mistake, and it cost them being received as authentic rap artists. A review of his album on RapReviews.com also points out that this was a good move. It allowed Cena to be seen as a rapper, rather than a wrestler who raps.

"Other than having his WWE title belt on the cover, you wouldn't really recognize he's a wrestler from listening to his rap," the review claims.

John Cena and his cousin, musical collaborator Tha Trademarc, sign copies of their rap album, *You Can't See Me*, for fans, May 12, 2005.

The album was all but ignored by rap radio stations. Still, dedicated WWE fans ensured that the album had a respectable debut at number 15 on the Billboard 200 and number 3 on the Billboard.biz Top Rap Album chart. This did not faze Cena at all. When asked in a *Men's Fitness* interview in 2005 what would happen if his album failed, he said it didn't really matter to him. He paid for the production of the album himself, and all the money he

John Cena has enjoyed success and fulfillment as an actor, but he claims he will never leave wrestling to act full time, as other wrestlers

would make from it went straight to the WWE. He wouldn't make a dime from it.

Lighting Up the Screen

Aside from rap, Cena has made a name for himself as an actor. He got his start on television, participating in a reality show called *Manhunt* in 2001. But most of his acting has been on the big screen. He made his first movie, *The Marine*, in 2006. He has since made three more films: *12 Rounds* in 2009, and *Legendary* and *Fred: The Movie* in 2010.

Cena's costar in his third movie, *Legendary*, was the very talented actress Patricia Clarkson. During a press junket interview just before the release of the film, he spoke about what it's like to work with professional actors. As reported by Eric Cohen on About.com, Cena compared working with Clarkson to being put in the New York Yankees lineup, using Nick

HOME LIFE

In spite of a busy WWE agenda that has him on the road almost constantly, John Cena has stayed true to his roots. He wed his high school sweetheart, Elizabeth Huberdeau, in July 2009 after a two-year engagement. They were married in Boston, and Cena's own father officiated the service. Prior to the wedding, Cena was very private about his dating life. There were rumors of various girlfriends, but it wasn't until 2007 that news of his engagement broke. He avoided fanfare and paparazzi by not revealing the plans for his wedding before the service. Even today, he is protective of his personal life in interviews, preferring to talk about himself as an athlete and performer and keeping his home life private. But marrying "the girl next door" is another indicator of how grounded Cena is. Even with all the money and fame and after traveling the world, he is loyal to his upbringing, to the person underneath all the riches.

Swisher as an example. Swisher wasn't a great player with the White Sox, but with the Yankees he became an MVP contender and an All-Star. Cena said this happened because Swisher was surrounded by greatness. When surrounded by people who are much better than you, you have two choices: you can give up, or you can step up and rise to the occasion. Cena said that being in scenes with someone as talented as Clarkson gave him no choice but to give it his all.

He says other wrestlers who have gone on to careers in acting did so because they could always picture life after wrestling, which he cannot. Cena famously and controversially criticized fellow wrestler turned actor the Rock for turning his back on wrestling once he made a name for himself in Hollywood. He accused the Rock of using wrestling as a platform for a career in acting, whereas for Cena wrestling has always been his focus. To him, there is no life after wrestling. He says if he weren't wrestling, he would probably just go back to mowing lawns. Cena is a wrestler at heart, and his fans can look forward to watching him dominate in the ring for a long time to come.

TIMELINE

1977– April 23, John Felix Anthony Cena is born in West Newbury, Massachusetts.

1989– Cena gets his first weight set at the age of twelve.

1998– Cena graduates from Springfield College, with a degree in exercise physiology.

1999– Cena moves to California to pursue a career in bodybuilding but becomes interested in wrestling.

2000– April 27, Cena, calling himself "the Prototype," captures the UPW title in San Diego, California.

2001– September 7, the UPN television show *Manhunt*, in which Cena stars, is canceled amid rumors that it is "fixed."

2002– June 27, Cena makes his television wrestling debut, answering a challenge from Kurt Angle.

2004– March 14, Cena defeats the Big Show to win the U.S. Championship in WrestleMania XX.

2004– July 8, he is stripped of the U.S. title due to accidentally hitting then-SmackDown general manager Kurt Angle.

2005– May 10, Cena's album, *You Can't See Me*, is released.

2005– August 14, cohosts the Teen Choice Awards with Hulk Hogan.

2006– October 13, *The Marine*, in which Cena stars, arrives in theaters.

2007– January 1, Cena wrestles Kevin Federline on the WWE's Raw and is pinned for a three count.

2007– October 2, Cena is stripped of the WWE Championship due to an injury.

2008– January 27, He makes an unannounced return, winning the Wrestle-Mania title shot.

2009– April 5, the twenty-fifth anniversary of WrestleMania; Cena defeats World Heavyweight Champion Edge and Big Show to win the title.

2009– July 11, Cena marries his childhood sweetheart, Elizabeth Huberdeau.

2010– September 10, the film *Legendary*, in which Cena stars, opens.

2010– November 22, Cena is fired from the WWE.

2011– January 1, Cena is nominated for ESPN SportsNation's first annual Awesomest Dude of the Year Award.

GLOSSARY

angle A fictional plot in wrestling.

bodybuilding Lifting weights to develop the muscles in the body.

face A wrestler who is liked and perceived as a nice guy.

feud A rivalry.

gimmick A trademark gesture or action that a wrestler becomes known for.

heel A wrestler who is disliked and perceived as a villain.

kayfabe The "secret" behind wrestling—that the storylines are fictional.

Olympic plates An intense form of weight lifting in which chains and other objects are used, rather than machines.

pectoral muscle A fan-shaped muscle in the chest area.

pin To hold an opponent's shoulders on the mat.

rookie A professional athlete in his or her first year.

steroids Drugs that boost athletic performance.

storyline A made-up plot line in wrestling.

stunts Acrobatics in wrestling, such as jumping or climbing objects.

Ultimate Pro Wrestling An independent wrestling organization.

Ultimate University A now-defunct training camp for WWE wrestlers.

WWE World Wrestling Entertainment.

WWF World Wrestling Federation.

Athletes Against Steroids

731 Kirkman Road

Orlando, FL 32811

(877) 914-9910

Web site: http://www.athletesagainststeroids.org

This organization is committed to discouraging athletes from using steroids and helping those who have already developed a dependency to quit using them.

Canadian Amateur Wrestling Association

7-5370 Canotek Road

Gloucester, ON K1J 9E6

Canada

(613) 748-5686

Web site: http://www.wrestling.ca

This organization encourages and develops the widest participation and highest proficiency in Olympic wrestling in Canada.

Hip Hop Association

545 8th Avenue, 10th Floor

New York, NY 10018

Web site: http://www.hiphopassociation.org

(718) 682-2744

This nonprofit organization fosters international social change through the use of media, popular culture, social entrepreneurship, leadership development, and diplomacy.

International Drug Free Athletics

P.O. Box 30007

RPO Brooklin Centre

Whitby, ON L1M 0B5

FOR MORE INFORMATION

Canada

(905) 655-4320

Web site: http://www.idfa.ca

This Canadian organization is committed to promoting drug-free bodybuilding worldwide through education, awareness, camaraderie, and community involvement.

Mothers Against Drunk Driving (MADD) National Office

511 E. John Carpenter Freeway, Suite 700

Irving, TX 75062

(800) GET-MADD [438-6233]

Web site: http://www.madd.org

MADD is committed to stopping drunk driving, supporting the victims of this violent crime, and preventing underage drinking.

National Center for Bullying Prevention

PACER Center, Inc.

8161 Normandale Boulevard

Bloomington, MN 55437

(888) 248-0822

Web site: http://www.pacer.org/bullying

This organization is dedicated to preventing the bullying of children.

Storm Wrestling Academy

P.O. Box 58013

Chaparral RPO

Calgary, AB T2X 3V2

Canada

Web site: http://academy.stormwrestling.com

This Canadian pro-wrestling school is operated and taught by former WWE superstar Lance Storm.

United Nations World Food Programme
Via C.G.Viola 68
Parco dei Medici
00148 Rome
Italy
Web site: http://www.wfp.org

This organization is dedicated to combating hunger worldwide. Will Smith and his wife, Jada Pinkett-Smith, are contributors.

Web Sites

Due to the changing nature of Internet links, Rosen Publishing has developed an online list of Web sites related to the subject of this book. This site is updated regularly. Please use this link to access the list:

http://www.rosenlinks.com/slam/jc

FOR FURTHER READING

Assael, Shaun. *Steroid Nation: Juiced Home Run Totals, Anti-Aging Miracles, and a Hercules in Every High School: The Secret History of America's True Drug Addiction.* New York, NY: ESPN, 2007.

Beekman, Scott. *Ringside: A History of Professional Wrestling in America.* Santa Barbara, CA: Praeger, 2006.

Brody, Howard. *Swimming with Piranhas: Surviving the Politics of Professional Wrestling.* Toronto, ON, Canada: ECW Press, 2009

Chang, Jeff. *Can't Stop Won't Stop: A History of the Hip-Hop Generation.* New York, NY: Picador, 2005.

Connors, Edward. *The Gold's Gym Encyclopedia of Bodybuilding.* New York, NY: McGraw-Hill, 1998.

Delavier, Frederic. *Strength Training Anatomy.* Champaign, IL: Human Kinetics, 2010.

Grayson, Robert. *John Cena: Modern Role Models.* Broomall, PA: Mason Crest Publishers, 2008.

Hogan, Hulk. *My Life Outside the Ring.* New York, NY: St. Martin's Press, 2009.

Jarman, Tom. *Wrestling for Beginners.* New York, NY: McGraw-Hill, 1983.

Jarmey, Chris. *The Concise Book of Muscles.* Berkeley, CA: North Atlantic Books, 2008.

Kennedy, Robert. *Encyclopedia of Bodybuilding: The Complete A–Z Book on Muscle Building.* Mississauga, ON, Canada: Robert Kennedy Publishing, 2008.

Kreidler, Mark. *Four Days to Glory: Wrestling with the Soul of the American Heartland.* New York, NY: Harper Paperbacks, 2007.

Martino, Alfred. *Pinned.* Boston, MA: Graphia, 2006.

Shields, Brian. *WWE Encyclopedia.* Indianapolis, IN: Brady Games, 2009.

Sitomer, Alan Lawrence, and Michael Cirelli. *Hip-Hop Poetry and the Classics.* Beverly Hills, CA: Milk Mug, 2004.

Sullivan, Kevin. *The WWE Championship: A Look Back at the Rich History of the WWE Championship.* Stamford, CT: WWE, 2010.

Vanilla Ice. *Ice by Ice: The Vanilla Ice Story in His Own Words.* New York, NY: Avon Books, 1991.

Wallace, Rich. *Winning Season.* London, England: Puffin, 2007.

Welker, William. *The Wrestling Drill Book.* Champaign, IL: Human Kinetics, 2005.

Zavoral, Nolan. *A Season on the Mat: Dan Gable and the Pursuit of Perfection.* New York, NY: Simon & Schuster, 2007.

BIBLIOGRAPHY

Caulfield, Keith. "WWE Champ Pins Hot Shot Bow." *Billboard*, May 28, 2005, Vol. 117, Issue 22, p. 47.

Cohen, Eric. "Jon Cena Interview at Legendary Press Junket." About. com. Retrieved February 10, 2011 (http://prowrestling.about.com/od/interviews/a/John-Cena-Interview.htm).

Fazende, Sean. "Jon Cena Louisiana SmackDown." Fox8-Live.com. Retrieved February 10, 2011 (http://www.fox8live.com/news/local/story/John-Cena-Louisiana-smackdown/Rz7Gl9pnLU2HbTKx_EuN4A.cspx).

John Cena interview. *Men's Fitness*, April 2005, Vol. 21, Issue 3, pp. 72–73.

Jones, Oliver. John Cena Interview. *People*, October 23, 2006, Vol. 66, Issue 17, p. 74.

Kamau, High. "A Cagey Match." *Billboard*, June 21, 2008, Vol. 120, Issue 25, p. 5.

Millado, Nate. "Unchained JC Cena." *Men's Fitness*, April 2009, Vol. 25, Issue 3, pp. 66–71.

Miller, Prairie. Interview with Jon Cena. *Long Island Press*, September 11, 2010. Retrieved February 10, 2011 (http://www.longislandpress.com/2010/09/11/interview-john-cena/1).

O'Connell, Jeff. "Armed & Dangerous." *Joe Weider's Muscle & Fitness*, November 2004, Vol. 65, Issue 11, pp. 94–99.

INDEX

About the Author

Tracy Brown has written several books for young adults on a variety of topics. With a son of her own, she is very interested in health and fitness issues for children, as well as encouraging healthy role models for boys. She lives in the Netherlands.

Photo Credits

Cover, p. 1 Tiziana Fabi/AFP/Getty Images; cover (background photo), p. 1 (background photo) Ethan Miller/Getty Images; p. 3 (boxing ring), chapter openers graphic (boxing ring) © www.istockphoto.com/Urs Siedentop; pp. 4–5 Moses Robinson/Getty Images; p. 7 (left) Mick Hutson/Redferns/Getty Images; p. 7 (right) Ron Galellea Ltd./Wirelmage/ Getty Images; p. 8 Will Hart/Getty Images Sport/Getty Images; pp. 10, 26, 33 Soul Brother/FilmMagic/Getty Images; p. 13 © AP Images; p. 14 Jam Media/LatinContent/ Getty Images; p. 17 © Copyright Fox Atomic. All rights reserved/courtesy Everett Collection; pp. 20, 23 KMazur/Wirelmage/Getty Images; p. 27 Zuma Press/Icon SMI; p. 30 Allen Kee/Wirelmage/Getty Images; pp. 34–35 © 20th Century Fox/Courtesy Everett Collection; cover background graphic, back cover background graphic, chapter openers background graphic, interior graphics Shutterstock.

Designer: Les Kanturek; Editor: Bethany Bryan; Photo Researcher: Marty Levick